HORSE RACING

HORSE RACING
THE GOLDEN AGE OF THE TRACK

PHOTOGRAPHS BY BERT MORGAN ★ INTRODUCTION BY BILL BARICH

EDITED BY ERIC RACHLIS AND BLOSSOM LEFCOURT

CHRONICLE BOOKS

SAN FRANCISCO

SPECIAL THANKS TO PHYLLIS ROGERS AND CATHY SCHENCK AT
THE KEENELAND LIBRARY FOR THEIR INVALUABLE ASSISTANCE.

LIBRARY OF CONGRESS CATALOGING-IN-PUBLICATION DATA AVAILABLE.

ISBN 0-8118-2990-1

PRINTED IN SINGAPORE.

DESIGNED BY HENRY QUIROGA.

DISTRIBUTED IN CANADA BY RAINCOAST BOOKS
9050 SHAUGHNESSY STREET
VANCOUVER, BRITISH COLUMBIA V6P 6E5

10 9 8 7 6 5 4 3 2 1

CHRONICLE BOOKS LLC
85 SECOND STREET
SAN FRANCISCO, CALIFORNIA 94105

WWW.CHRONICLEBOOKS.COM

ADDITIONAL PHOTO CAPTIONS:

Front cover: Finish line of the first triple dead heat in horse racing history, at Aqueduct Racecourse, Jamaica, NY, June 10, 1944.

p. 2: Jockey Johnny Longden.

p. 3: Assault, Warren Mehrtens up, after winning the 1946 Triple Crown.

p. 4: The Wood Memorial race, Jamaica Park racetrack, Jamaica, NY, April 20, 1957, won by Bold Ruler (right), Eddie Arcaro up.

pp. 8–9: Count Fleet, Johnny Longden up, racing to win the Wood Memorial Race at Jamaica Park racetrack, Jamaica, NY, April 17, 1943.

p. 10: The finish line, Belmont Park, Long Island, NY, June 7, 1941. First place is Whirlaway, Eddie Arcaro up; second is Robert Morris, Alfred Robertson up; third is Yankee Chance, Basil B. James up; fourth is Itabo, Earl H. Bierman up.

pp. 12–13: Count Fleet, winning the 1943 Belmont Stakes by twenty-five lengths (visible far behind is the second-place horse, Fairy Manhunt).

Back cover: View of the crowd on opening day at the Jamaica Park racetrack, Jamaica, NY, April 8, 1943.

★★★ PREFACE ★★★

Bert Morgan was born in 1904 in Lancashire county, in northern England, and was raised just down the road from Aintree Racecourse, site of the Grand National. At age seven, he and his family moved to Brooklyn, New York, and at fifteen he was working with his older brother syndicating photographs for the *Chicago Tribune* and the *New York Daily News*. Then, in 1930, he began taking his own photographs with a camera he bought for a quarter.

He quickly became a freelance candid photographer of high society, whose work also appeared in *Vogue, Vanity Fair, Town & Country, Women's Wear Daily*, and other periodicals. Because many high-society figures were involved in the thoroughbred industry, Bert regularly took photographs of Triple Crown races and at flat and steeple-chase races along the eastern seaboard from New York to Florida. In 1940, Bert was appointed the New York Racing Association's official track photographer. Throughout his twenty-one-year career with the NYRA he was an innovator of equine photography, popularizing unusual angles for photographs, such as shooting from nearly head-on and from beneath the inside rail, and lending a new excitement to race photography. In one such innovative shot, included in this book on pp.12–13, Morgan captures both the winning horse, Count Fleet, and the second-place horse, Fairy Manhunt, a distant twenty-five lengths behind. His work earned him the first-ever George B. Featherston photojournalism award for excellence in equine photography by the *Thoroughbred Record.*

His son, Richard, born in 1936, began assisting him at racetracks in New York and on other assignments; in 1956 they formed the Bert and Richard Morgan Studio, going on to photograph Triple Crown races for the next fifty-five years.

In 1994, Archive Photos acquired exclusive worldwide representation rights to the Bert and Richard Morgan Collection. This book showcases the glamour and excitement of the racing world that Bert Morgan's photographs uniquely capture.

—Eric Rachlis
Archive Photos

★★★ INTRODUCTION ★★★

WE GO TO THE RACETRACK in search of the unexpected, so it shouldn't come as a surprise to stumble on a picture of Mamie Eisenhower posed by the rail at Belmont Park. Dressed in a pillbox hat, a net veil, and white gloves, she consults her program with a sly smile, while her husband looks on. Does Mamie have a lock on the daily double, and will she share it with Ike? Note that her program shows signs of actual use. It curls at the edges, as if she'd rolled it up and stuffed it into a back pocket, just as veteran punters do. And how did Mamie react when the horses crossed the wire? Did she jump for joy, or curse and tear up her ticket? That must remain a mystery forever, because the celebrities and society folks in Bert Morgan's photographs never lose their composure.

Morgan didn't document the ordinary world of the track. There are no tears shed, no lame horses, filthy grooms, or crooked trainers. Instead, he concentrated on those moments when racing rose to its zenith, and the rich and famous dropped out of the sky to take in the Belmont Stakes or the Kentucky Derby. His images are alive with a stylish elegance. The men's trousers always have razor-sharp creases, and the women may be excused for wearing a fur piece in May. The Whitneys, the Vanderbilts, Black Jack Bouvier, Prince Aly Khan—they are caught in perfect sunlight as they move from the paddock to the grandstand in the most expensive and fashionable clothes around.

They give off a vibration of health and well-being, of European spas, fine hotels, gin gimlets, and old money. In the closed circle of privilege, they might brush up against Babe Ruth and George Raft at the pari-mutuel windows, or stop in at the Turf Club for a quick cocktail with Bing Crosby.

Once, horse racing truly was the Sport of Kings, and Bert Morgan had the good luck to be on the beat during the glory years. His career as the official photographer for the New York Racing Association stretched roughly from the mid-1930s into the 1950s, at a time when playing the ponies was as popular as attending a ball game or a boxing match. You can see this in Morgan's photo of opening day at Jamaica Park, in April of 1943. The grounds are as packed as midtown Manhattan at rush hour. Indeed, the presence of so many gents in business suits suggests that not a few of them ducked out of the office early to be on hand. Or consider the gang jammed into the betting ring at Belmont, in 1933. The stock market had crashed only four years earlier, but you'd never know it. Our boys can't wait to make a wager. In a sea of hats, they swarm toward a row of bookies, who chalk the ever-changing odds on slates and probably go home happier than most of their customers.

The crowd pictures have a palpable sense of excitement. Everyone's slightly on edge, because if you blinked in those days you could miss the whole show. There were no closed-circuit TVs or instant replays. Racing was just emerging from its infancy and entering an era of new technologies. The starting gate, for instance, came into general use in 1929. Until 1932, when Joseph Widener, the heir to a streetcar fortune, introduced saliva tests, horses could easily be doped or even poisoned. Widener was also responsible for the totalizator board, an invention borrowed from the Australians. In 1936, the photo-finish camera was added to the machinery, and its immediate effect was to bring into question the nature of reality and produce a rash of dead heats. Moreover, the breeding operations of the so-called "horsey set" were kicking into high gear. It was a flourishing, optimistic period, and the photographs reflect that spirit.

Seen through Morgan's eyes, the racetrack is strikingly romantic. It has a kind of grandeur, even an epic quality. The horses, too, are blessed with a heroic dimension. Take Man o' War, for example, who won twenty of his twenty-one races, although he ran in heavy iron shoes and carried as much as 138 pounds in one handicap. (His single loss, at Saratoga, involved a bad start.) "Big Red," as he was known, lived to be thirty and became a symbol of American force and durability, so beloved that his birthday party was once broadcast to the nation on NBC Radio. Then there is Citation, who took the Triple Crown in 1948, despite competing in twenty races that year. He had tendon problems as a four-year-old and rested for a season, but he returned at five and six and went on to be the track's first million-dollar winner, finishing in the money in forty-four of forty-five contests.

In fact, only ten colts have won the Triple Crown since Sir Barton first did it in 1919, and Morgan photographed six of them, serving up a dynasty of equine royalty as distinguished as the aristocratic families that created it. His portraits are wonderful for their variety. Rather than repeat the standard winner's circle shot, he improvised and found ways to bring out the character of each different horse. Although Assault, Whirlaway, and Count Fleet never achieved the imperial status of Man o' War, the fans still clipped their pictures from the paper and followed their exploits as closely as those of Joe Louis or the Brooklyn Dodgers. In sporting terms, it was an era of relative simplicity, and the top stars in any game had wide public recognition, including such legendary trainers as "Sunny Jim" Fitzsimmons and Ben Jones of Calumet Farm,

along with the great jockey Eddie Arcaro, who rode five Derby winners and twice won the Triple Crown.

No golden age lasts forever, of course. Racing began to lose some of its shine toward the end of Morgan's tenure and assumed a far less prominent position on the social calendar. The crowds thinned out, too, as the competition for recreational dollars turned more intense. Up against televised sports and casino gambling, the tracks watched their handle fall and their patrons grow older. Today the average facility must rely on simulcast races and exotic wagering to stay afloat, but for the Pick Six to attract bettors and generate a lottery-size payoff, you need large fields. Those fields are often fleshed out with inferior horses, especially at cheap tracks.

Still, there are times when you catch glimpses of the racetrack as Bert Morgan saw it, elegant and formal, a universe of bright surfaces where honor, decorum, and order prevail. August in Saratoga still has the atmosphere of a country idyll, with its own subset of galas, dinners, parties, and dances to provide material for the columnists. The bougainvillea at Hialeah may not bloom so lavishly anymore, but you can still sit in a rattan armchair on a terrace and enjoy the Florida sunshine in winter, as Joe, Rose, and Jackie Kennedy did. And on Derby Day at Churchill Downs, the choice grandstand seats still go to the movers and shakers, while the millinery display is as grand as ever. In the end, it's a pretty bubble we have before us in this book, one that combines class and innocence in ideal measure.

—*Bill Barich*

June 5, 1943

Blue Peter, trained by Andy Schuttinger, owned by Joseph M. Roebling,
Belmont Park, Long Island, NY, September 28, 1948.

Man o' War with trainer Will Harbutt, July 21, 1945.

Man o' War, July 21, 1945.

War Admiral, winner of the 1937 Triple Crown, owned by Samuel D. Riddle, trained by George Conway, at Aqueduct Racecourse, Jamaica, NY, June 17, 1937.

Triple Crown winner Whirlaway, owned by Warren Wright
of Calumet Farm, trained by Ben A. Jones, at Hialeah Park,
Hialeah, FL, February 14, 1941.

Bold, winner of the Preakness, owned by Mrs. I. D. Sloane of Brookemeade
Stable, pictured with Mr. Preston Burch, Mr. Elliot Burch, and Mr. Clarence
Parish at Belmont Park, Long Island, NY, June 4, 1951.

(Left to right) Bold Ruler; Independence, Thomas Walsh holding reins; and Three Full Brothers at Saratoga Race Course, Saratoga Springs, NY, August 13, 1958.

Bull Lea, Eddie Arcaro up, at the Grand Union Hotel Stakes, Saratoga Race Course, Saratoga, NY, August 21, 1937.

Citation, Albert Snider up, going to post at the Futurity Stakes, Belmont Park, Long Island, NY, October 4, 1947. Citation won the 1948 Triple Crown.

Bold, winner of the Preakness, owned by Mrs. I. D. Sloane of
Brookmeade Stable, at Belmont Park, Long Island, NY, June 4, 1951.

Horses coming in from the paddock at Saratoga Race Course, Saratoga Springs, NY, 1930s.

(Left to right) Mrs. Kennedy Molton, Alfred G. Vanderbilt, and Mrs. Cartwright Wetherill at Belmont Park, Long Island, NY, 1950s.

Mr. and Mrs. Cornelius Vanderbilt Whitney at Meadow Brook Cup Races, probably in NY, 1930s.

Mrs. Robert L. Stevens and Prince Serge Obolensky at Belmont Park, Long Island, NY, 1930s.

Mrs. P. A. B. Widener and Mr. Joseph E. Widener, of the Savoy Plaza Hotel in NYC, at Belmont Park, Long Island, NY, 1934.

Bing Crosby at the Belmont Opening, 1933.

John M. Gaver and John Hay Whitney at Belmont Park, Long Island, NY, 1946.

Public auction horse sale, Belmont Park, Long Island, NY, 1947. George Swinebroad, auctioneer; Humphrey Finney, director of sales.

Morty Lynch, bookmaker, 1930s.

Totalizator board at Hialeah Park, Hialeah, FL, 1930s.

Crowd at the Kentucky Derby by the pari-mutuel board, Churchill Downs, Louisville, KY, 1930s.

The betting ring at Belmont Park, Long Island, NY, May 1935.

George Raft at Belmont Park, Long Island, NY, September 18, 1941.

Raymond Guest, Thomas Hitchcock Jr., George H. "Pete" Bostwick, and Earle W. Hopping sit on a bench at Belmont Park, Long Island, NY, 1935.

Front row (left to right): President and Mrs. Dwight D. Eisenhower, Mrs. George D. Widener, Mr. and Mrs. John W. Hanes, and Mr. Jerry O'Grady; back (left): Mr. Edward T. Dickinson and Mrs. Robert J. Kleberg, walking past spectators at Belmont Park, Long Island, NY, June 3, 1961.

John V. Bouvier III and his daughter C. Lee Bouvier (now wife of Polish Prince Stanislaus Radziwill). Belmont Park, Long Island, NY, June 12, 1948.

J. Barney Balding greets Mrs. George Bostwick, with Albert Bostwick, Belmont Park, Long Island, NY, May 12, 1942.

Elizabeth Taylor at Hialeah Park, Hialeah, FL, 1950s.

(Left to right) Mrs. John C. Clark, Mrs. Daniel R. Topping, and Mrs. Jacqueline Kennedy (holding a clubhouse return check), at Hialeah Park, Hialeah, FL, 1955.

Mr. John Sanford and trainer Hollie Hughes at Belmont Park, Long Island, NY, June 1936.

Mr. and Mrs. Joseph P. Kennedy, consulting the racing form at Hialeah Park, Hialeah, FL, 1954.

Mr. Edward Riley Bradley and Mrs. Elizabeth Altemus Whitney reviewing the racing form at Saratoga Race Course, Saratoga Springs, NY, August 8, 1942.

Standing at railing (left to right): Mr. Robert J. Kleberg Jr., President and Mrs. Dwight D. Eisenhower, Mrs. George M. Humphrey, Mrs. George D. Widener, Mrs. John W. Hanes, and Mr. George M. Humphrey at Belmont Park, Long Island, NY, June 3, 1961.

President and Mrs. Dwight D. Eisenhower consult a racing bill, Belmont Park, Long Island, NY, June 3, 1961.

Jacqueline Bouvier at Memorial Day celebrations at the Turf and Field Club, Belmont Park, Long Island, NY, May 30, 1939.

George Herman "Babe" Ruth at Belmont Park, Long Island, NY, July 19, 1947.

Mrs. Stephen Sanford of Kings Point, Long Island, NY, and Mrs. Charles B. Wrightsman of Westbury, Long Island, NY, at Hialeah Park, Hialeah, FL, early 1940s.

New York Governor Averill Harriman and F. Skiddy von Stade, president of Saratoga Race Course, Saratoga Springs, NY, August 16, 1955.

The crowd and band at Jamaica Park racetrack, Jamaica, NY, April 12, 1941.

Native Dancer, Eric Guerin up, the Belmont Stakes, Belmont Park, Long Island, NY, June 13, 1953.

Count Fleet, Johnny Longden up, trained by Don Cameron, at the Kentucky Derby, Churchill Downs, Louisville, KY, May 2, 1943.

Whirlaway, Alfred Robertson up, trained by Ben A. Jones and owned by
Calumet Farm, Belmont Park, Long Island, NY, 1941.

Jay Jay, Harry Richards up, winner of the American Legion Handicap, Saratoga Race Course, Saratoga Springs, NY, July 26, 1937.

Old Grad, William Cummings up, at Aqueduct Racecourse, Jamaica, NY, July 9, 1945.

Jet Pilot, Eric Guerin up, owned by Tom Smith of the Maine Chance Farm, at Belmont Park, Long Island, NY, May 17, 1947.

Harlequin, L. Veitch up, at Aqueduct Racecourse, Jamaica, NY, late 1930s. Horse owned by Robert Pinkerton Gibb.

Triple Crown winner War Admiral, Charles Kurtsinger up, owned by Samuel D. Riddle of Glen Riddle Farms, 1937.

Old Grad, William Cummings up, at Aqueduct Racecourse, Jamaica, NY, July 9, 1945.

Triple Crown winner Assault, Eddie Arcaro up, owned by R. J. Kleberg, trained by Max Hirsch,
Belmont Park, Long Island, NY, September 27, 1947.

Hurdle race, with view of the field and grandstand, at Belmont Park, Long Island, NY, June 3, 1953.
#8—Sir Ronald II (in the middle of the pack), Ramon Harris up—won the race.

The Quogue at Belmont Park, Long Island, NY, May 25, 1937. The rearing horse is Flying Dove, James Stout up, owned by W. H. La Boyteaux.

Daggers Drawn, Wayne D. Wright up, rearing up at the start of a race at Belmont Park, Long Island, NY, May 25, 1937.

The first use of the "Wait Jr." starting gate on any track, the first race at Aqueduct Racecourse, Jamaica, NY, June 10, 1935.

Start of the first race, won by Knows Peace (#14), at Saratoga Race Course, Saratoga Springs, NY, August 27, 1951.

Start of the Belmont Stakes, Belmont Park, Long Island, NY, June 13, 1953.

Start of a race, Aqueduct Racecourse, Jamaica, NY, date unknown.

Start of a race at Empire City racetrack, Yonkers, NY, date unknown.

President and Mrs. Dwight D. Eisenhower spectating from inside a viewing booth at Aqueduct Racecourse, Jamaica, NY, October 19, 1961.

Mrs. John A. Morris and Mrs. Cornelius Vanderbilt Whitney, enjoying the races at Saratoga Race Course, Saratoga Springs, NY, 1950s.

The Stymie Stakes, Belmont Park, Long Island, NY, June 25, 1958. First—Bold Ruler, Eddie Arcaro up, wearing the Wheatley Stable colors, owned by Mrs. Henry Carnegie Phipps, trained by James E. "Sunny Jim" Fitzsimmons; second—Admiral Vee; third—Pop Corn.

View from the top of the grandstand, Belmont Park, Long Island, NY, September 26, 1941.

View of crowd on opening day at Jamaica Park racetrack, Jamaica, NY, April 8, 1943.

Race finish at Belmont Park,
Long Island, NY, 1930s.

(Left to right) Lt. Gen. Hugh A. Drum, Rear Adm. Edward J. Marquart, and Maj. Gen. Irving J. Phillipson, Belmont Park, Long Island, NY, November 5, 1942.

Mrs. Winston Guest (right) and an unidentified woman, in a private box at Saratoga Race Course, Saratoga Springs, NY, 1954.

(Left to right) Edith Roark, Tommy Manville, and Dolly Goering, standing at the rail at the Kentucky Derby, Churchill Downs, Louisville, KY, May 8, 1937.

Mrs. John V. Bouvier III (left) with Mrs. John J. Ryan Jr., in the stands at Belmont Park, Long Island, NY, May 9, 1938.

Finish of the sixth race at Aqueduct Racecourse, Jamaica, NY, September 14, 1944. First—Old Grad, Robert Permane up; second—Might Master, Francis J. Maschek up; third—Dove Shoot, Eric Guerin up.

Unidentified horse and jockey at the Rosetree Hunter
Challenge Cup, Rosetree racetrack, Media, PA, 1930s.

Knight Alert, James Murphy up, in the lead at Aqueduct Racecourse, Jamaica, NY, June 22, 1953.

Race at Belmont Park, Long Island, NY, June 10, 1953, #2—Springdale, Charles Harr up; #1—Escarp, Thomas McFarland up; #6—Henrico, Ramon Harris up; #7—Mailing List, Elwood Carter up.

Belmont Park, Long Island, NY, June 10, 1953. #3—Spleen, Melvin Ferrall up; #1—Escarp, Thomas McFarlane up; #6—Henrico, Ramon Harris up.

The Tourist Handicap, the second race at Belmont Park, Long Island, NY, June 11, 1953. #6–Montadent, Flint Schulhofer up, owned by John M. Schiff, trained by O. T. Dubassoff.

The Roseben Handicap at Belmont Park, Long Island, NY, 1943, won by #1—Some Chance, Joe Renick up.

The Wood Memorial Race, Jamaica Park, Jamaica, NY, April 20, 1957. Winner (right) Bold Ruler, Eddie Arcaro up; Gallant Man (left) was second; Promised Land (back), third.

Finish of the Match Race at Pimlico Race Course, Baltimore, MD, November 1, 1938. First—Seabiscuit, George Woolf up, Tom Smith owner and trainer; second—War Admiral, Charles Kurtsinger up. Note the hat thrown into the air at right.

The finish line, Belmont Park, Long Island, NY, June 7, 1941. First place is Whirlaway, Eddie Arcaro up; second is Robert Morris, Alfred Robertson up; third is Yankee Chance, Basil B. James up; fourth is Itabo, Earl H. Bierman up.

Triple Crown winner Assault winning the 1946 Kentucky Derby.

THE KENTUCKY DERB
"SPY SONG", 2ND. "HAMPDEN
1¼ MILES - 2:06 3

3RD.

Belmont Park Match Race finish, Belmont Park, Long Island, NY, September 23, 1941. In first place was Alsab, Bobby Vedder up, owned by Mrs. A. Sabath; in second place was Requested, Jack G. Westrope up, owned by B. F. Whitaker.

Finish of the sixty-seventh Kentucky Derby, with a new record time of 2:01, set May 3, 1941.
First—Whirlaway, Eddie Arcaro up, Calumet Farm owner; second—Staretor, George Woolf up,
H. S. Nesbitt owner; third—Market Wise, Irving Anderson up, L. Tufano owner.

Teletime board, Belmont Park, Long Island, NY, May 27, 1943.

		win	place	show
"THE CARTER HANDICAP"	#6 BROWNIE —	$2.40	2.30	2.30
$10,000 ADDED	#1 BOSSUET —	3.50	3.40	3.70
Triple Dead Heat for "WIN"	#3 WAIT-A-BIT —	4.30	3.90	3.90
TIME 1:23⅖ ★ 7 FURLONGS				

Finish line of the first triple dead heat in horse racing history, at Aqueduct Racecourse, Jamaica, NY, June 10, 1944. In order of their placing in the race: #1–Bossuet, James Stout up; #3–Wait-a-Bit, Gayle Loyal Smith up; #6–Brownie, Eric Guerin up.

Blue Peter, owned by J. M. Roebling, winner of the fifth race at the Futurity, Belmont Park, Long Island, NY, September 25, 1948, pictured with trainer Andy Schuttinger and jockey Eric Guerin.

Mrs. Silas B. Mason leading Head Play, Charles Kurtsinger up, after winning the Suburban Handicap at Belmont Park, Long Island, NY, 1935.

E. R. Bradley leading Black Helen, Don Meade up, after the Coaching Club American Oaks at Belmont Park, Long Island, NY, 1935.

Mrs. John Hay Whitney leads Singing Wood, Robert Jones up, winner of the Futurity Stakes at Belmont Park, Long Island, NY, 1933.

Presentation on the occasion of the retirement of Bold Ruler, standing in the background. Trainer James E. "Sunny Jim" Fitzsimmons (far left) and jockey Eddie Arcaro (left), with John W. Hanes and Ogden Phipps.

Jockey Club Gold Cup, Belmont Park, Long Island, NY, October 1, 1938. War Admiral, Wayne D. Wright up, owned by Samuel D. Riddle of Glen Riddle Farms, trained by George Conway.

Bolivar, James Stout up, owned by Belair Stud, at the Cocktail Party Sweepstakes, June 14, 1941.

Granville, James Stout up, at Saratoga Race Course, Saratoga Springs, NY, August 15, 1936.

The Kentucky Derby, Churchill Downs, Louisville, KY, May 8, 1937. Winner (and Triple Crown winner) War Admiral, Charles Kurtsinger up, owned by Samuel D. Riddle of Glen Riddle Farms.

Handcuff, I. Hanford up, winner of the Wakefield Handicap, Empire City racetrack, Yonkers, NY, July 24, 1937.

Winner's circle, Belmont Park, Long Island, NY, May 22, 1943. Count Fleet, Johnny Longden up, owner Mrs. John D. Hertz holding horse, Don Cameron trainer. The win secured Count Fleet the Triple Crown.

(Left to right) Charles E. Wacker III, John W. Hanes, Prince Aly Khan, C. Z. Guest, and Winston Guest standing by the track at Aqueduct Racecourse, Jamaica, NY, 1950s.

Charles Scribner and C. Douglass Dillon each hold a handle of the Wilmerding Cup in Far Hills, NJ, 1940s.

Belmont Stakes, Belmont Park, Long Island, NY, June 7, 1941. Whirlaway, Eddie Arcaro up, with trainer Ben A. Jones (holding horse), owned by Warren Wright (not shown).

Presentation to Samuel D. Riddle, owner, and jockey Charles Kurtsinger, following War Admiral's win of the Belmont Stakes, Belmont Park, Long Island, NY, June 5, 1937.

Winner's circle at the Kentucky Derby, Churchill Downs, Louisville, KY, May 4, 1946. Assault, Warren Mehrtens up, owned by King Ranch.

The Champagne Stakes, Belmont Park, Long Island, NY, October 4, 1941. The winner, Alsab, Earl H. Bierman up, owned by Mrs. A. Sabath of Chicago. Alsab would go on to win The Preakness in 1942.

Jockey Grover Stephens at Rosetree racetrack, Media, PA, May 21, 1949.

Jockey William "Bill" Hartack, Belmont Park,
Long Island, NY, September 22, 1954.

Jockeys Basil James, Alfred Robertson, and Rupert Donoso at Saratoga Race Course, Saratoga Springs, NY, July 23, 1941.

Jockey Joe Renick in Binglin Stock Farm colors (Bing Crosby's farm), with trainer William Post after winning the Suburban Handicap with horse Don Bingo, Belmont Park, Long Island, NY, May 31, 1943.

Jockeys at Belmont Park,
Long Island, NY, 1930s.

Jockey Rigan McKinney, leading amateur steeplechase rider, at Saratoga Race Course, Saratoga Springs, NY, 1937.

Jockeys Mike and Pat Smithwick, Rosetree racetrack, Media, PA, May 21, 1949.

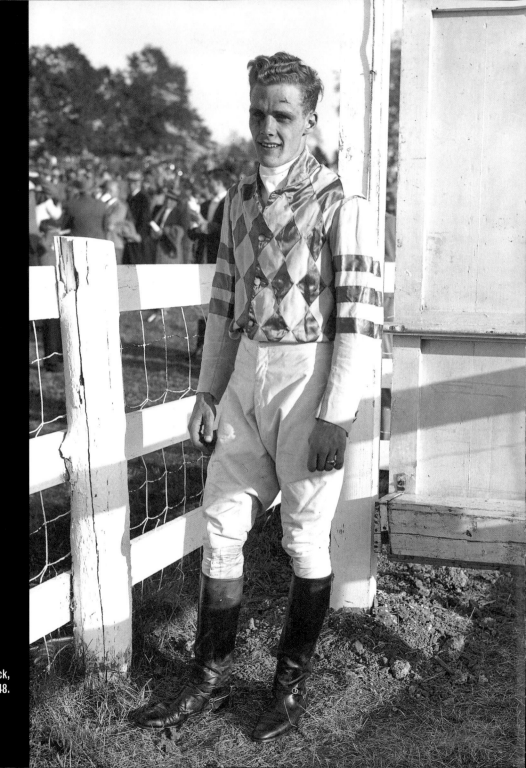

Jockey Grover Stephens at Far Hills racetrack,
New Jersey, October 30, 1948.

Kaster, Catalano up, at Saratoga Race Course,
Saratoga Springs, NY, August 4, 1953.

Fenlon, James Stout up, winner of the New York Handicap, Belmont Park, Long Island, NY, October 4, 1941.

Blue Peter, winner of the fifth race at the Futurity Stakes, Belmont Park, Long Island, NY, September 25, 1948,
pictured with trainer Andy Schuttinger and jockey Eric Guerin, owned by Joseph M. Roebling.

Don Bingo, Joe Renick up, with trainer William Post after winning the Suburban Handicap, Belmont Park, Long Island, NY, May 31, 1943.

Bing Crosby with the reins of his horse, Don Bingo, Alfred Robertson up; trainer William Post is behind Crosby at right; Belmont Park, Long Island, NY, May 26, 1943.

Rewing, Scott D. Riles up, winner of the third race at Aqueduct Racecourse, Jamaica, NY, June 23, 1953. Owner Mrs. R. Wingfield.

Omaha, Wayne D. Wright up, owned by William Woodward, trained by James E. "Sunny Jim" Fitzsimmons, at Aqueduct Racecourse, Jamaica, NY, 1935. Omaha won the 1935 Triple Crown.

Gallant Man, Willie Shoemaker up, Ralph Lowe owner,
John A. Nerud trainer, at the Nassau County Handicap
at Belmont Park, Long Island, NY, September 18, 1957.

The Suburban Handicap, Belmont Park, Long Island, NY, May 31, 1943.